TEAM SPIRIT ®

SMART BOOKS FOR YOUNG FANS

THE ARIZONA CARDINALS

BY
MARK STEWART

New Hanover County Public Library
201 Chestnut Street
Wilmington, North Carolina 28401

NORWOOD HOUSE PRESS

CHICAGO, ILLINOIS

Norwood House Press
P.O. Box 316598
Chicago, Illinois 60631

For information regarding Norwood House Press, please visit our website at:
www.norwoodhousepress.com or call 866-565-2900.

All photos courtesy of Getty Images except the following:
Icon SMI (4, 14, 27), Topps, Inc. (6, 9, 11, 21, 23, 35 top left, 40, 43 top & bottom right), Little Brown (7),
Black Book Partners (10, 18, 19, 25, 35 top right, 42 bottom), Ziff Davis Publishing Company (15),
Bowman Gum Co. (16, 17, 36), Cardinals/NFL (20, 22, 31, 37, 38, 45),
Goal Line Art, Inc. (24, 30), Author's Collection (33), TCMA Ltd. (42 top left),
Xerographics Inc. (42 bottom left), Matt Richman (48).
Cover Photo: Icon SMI.

The memorabilia and artifacts pictured in this book are presented for educational and informational purposes,
and come from the collection of the author.

Editor: Mike Kennedy
Designer: Ron Jaffe
Project Management: Black Book Partners, LLC.
Special thanks to Topps, Inc.

Library of Congress Cataloging-in-Publication Data

Stewart, Mark, 1960-
  The Arizona Cardinals / by Mark Stewart.
     p. cm. -- (Team spirit)
  Includes bibliographical references and index.
  Summary: "A revised Team Spirit Football edition featuring the Arizona
Cardinals that chronicles the history and accomplishments of the team.
Includes access to the Team Spirit website which provides additional
information and photos"--Provided by publisher.
  ISBN 978-1-59953-512-8 (library edition : alk. paper) -- ISBN
978-1-60357-454-9 (ebook) 1. Arizona Cardinals (Football
team)--History--Juvenile literature. I. Title.
  GV956.A75S84 2012
  796.332'640979173--dc23
                                          2012020037

Manufactured in the United States of America in North Mankato, Minnesota.
205N—082012

COVER PHOTO: The Cardinals are one of football's most exciting teams. Every touchdown brings a big celebration.

Table of Contents

ABOUT OUR GLOSSARY

In this book, there may be several words that you are reading for the first time. Some are sports words, some are new vocabulary words, and some are familiar words that are used in an unusual way. All of these words are defined on page 46. Throughout the book, sports words appear in **bold type**. Regular vocabulary words appear in ***bold italic type***.

Meet the Cardinals

How many teams in the **National Football League (NFL)** can say they are older than the state they play in? The Arizona Cardinals can. Their roots trace back to 1898, or 14 years before Arizona joined the United States.

The Cardinals actually began in Chicago, Illinois. They also spent many years in St. Louis, Missouri. Arizona is their third home. Along the way, the Cardinals learned what it takes to be a championship team.

This book tells the story of the Cardinals. They have had plenty of superstars over the years. They have also found talented **role players** who do all the little things that help a team win. In the seasons when the Cardinals put it all together, they have been something to behold. Even in defeat, Arizona still manages to be one of the NFL's most breathtaking teams. Win or lose, there is rarely a dull moment when the Cardinals play.

The Cardinals celebrate a touchdown. They can score from anywhere on the field.

Glory Days

mericans were first introduced to football in the 1800s. Back then, the sport was played mostly by men in their teens and early 20s. They took the field for fun and glory. In the 1890s, a few teams began charging fans to watch them play. This was the beginning of *professional* football. Chicago was home to one of the first pro teams. The players wore red jerseys, and the team became known as the Cardinals.

ALL AMERICAN

STANFORD

ERNIE NEVERS *Fullback*

Soon there was enough interest in pro football to form an entire league. In 1920, the Cardinals joined forces with 13 other clubs in the **American Professional Football Association (APFA)**. Two years later, it was renamed the NFL. The Cardinals' chief rivals were the Bears, who also played in Chicago.

The Cardinals won their first championship in 1925. Their leader was a great runner and kicker named Paddy Driscoll. In the years that followed, the Cardinals welcomed many more stars, including Ernie Nevers and Duke Slater. Nevers was the best all-around player in the NFL. He once scored 40 points in a game against the Bears. Slater was an excellent blocker and tackler—and the top African-American player of his time.

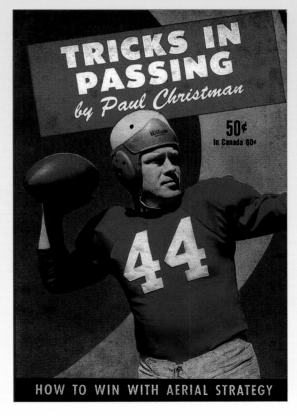

After many losing seasons in the 1930s, the Cardinals returned to the top of football in the years after **World War II**. They beat the Philadelphia Eagles for the 1947 NFL championship. A year later, Chicago lost in a rematch with the Eagles. Quarterback Paul Christman and running backs Pat Harder, Elmer Angsman, and Charley Trippi formed the heart of these teams. They were nicknamed the "Million Dollar Backfield."

All along, the Cardinals and Bears competed for the hearts of Chicago fans. In the end, after nearly 40 seasons, the Bears won

LEFT: This trading card shows Ernie Nevers during his college days.
ABOVE: Quarterback Paul Christman wrote the book on passing!

out. In 1960, the Cardinals moved to St. Louis. The team thrilled fans in its new home during the next *decade*. On offense, Charley Johnson was one of the most talented passers in the league. Jackie Smith, Sonny Randle, and Bobby Joe Conrad were sure-handed receivers. The St. Louis defense was fast and unpredictable. It starred Larry Wilson, who made tackles all over the field.

The Cardinals were even better during the mid-1970s. Their coach was Don Coryell. He was a genius when it came to the passing game. Coryell put together a great offense that included quarterback Jim Hart, receivers Mel Gray and Roy Green, kicker Jim Bakken, and running back Terry Metcalf. In 1979, Ottis Anderson joined the team. In his first year, he ran for 1,605 yards and was named the Offensive **Rookie** of the Year. Even with all this talent, St. Louis fell short of reaching the **Super Bowl**.

In 1988, the team moved again, this time to Arizona. The fans there were hungry for pro football and supported the Cardinals with great *enthusiasm*. Over the next decade, the team put some

LEFT: Ottis Anderson takes on the defense of the New York Giants.
ABOVE: Jackie Smith was one of the NFL's best tight ends.

terrific young players on the field, including Aeneas Williams, Larry Centers, Eric Swann, Simeon Rice, Jake Plummer, Rob Moore, and Pat Tillman. They helped the Cardinals get back to the **playoffs**.

More change greeted the Cardinals in 2002. For years, they had been part of the **East Division** of the **National Football Conference (NFC)**. Now Arizona switched to the **NFC West**. The change helped the Cardinals start new *rivalries* that energized the fans.

In 2005, quarterback Kurt Warner joined the team. He formed a dangerous passing combination with receivers Anquan Boldin and Larry Fitzgerald. That season, they each caught more than 100 passes. The Cardinals had a losing record, but they were one of the most exciting teams in the league.

Two years later, Arizona hired Ken Whisenhunt to coach the team. He had helped the Pittsburgh Steelers win the Super Bowl as an assistant coach a few years earlier. Whisenhunt used his championship experience to rebuild the Cardinals.

In just his second season, Whisenhunt guided the Cardinals to the Super Bowl for the first time in team history. Warner, Boldin, and Fitzgerald were still the stars on offense. The defense, meanwhile,

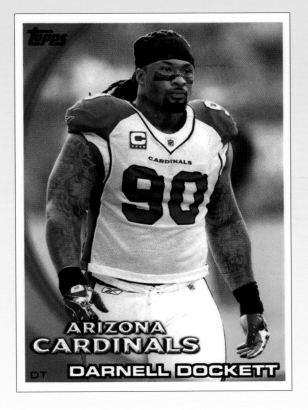

had improved, thanks to **Pro Bowl** players such as Adrian Wilson, Dominique Rodgers-Cromartie, and Darnell Dockett. Arizona added more difference-makers on defense in the years that followed. In 2011, the Cardinals drafted defensive back Patrick Peterson. He was named **All-Pro** as a rookie. That same year, Beanie Wells ran for more than 1,000 yards. With a taste of success and a winning *tradition* in place, one of pro football's oldest clubs felt like a new team—and was ready to win its first Super Bowl!

LEFT: Anquan Boldin sets his sights on the end zone.
ABOVE: Darnell Dockett helped Arizona reach the Super Bowl.

Home Turf

For most of their time in Chicago, the Cardinals shared Comiskey Park with the White Sox baseball team. They also hosted games at Soldier Field, which was later used by the Bears. In St. Louis, the Cardinals played in Busch Stadium, which was also the home of the Cardinals baseball team.

After moving to Arizona, the Cardinals played on college fields. In 2006, the Cardinals moved into a modern stadium of their own. The field is covered by a dome with a *retractable* roof. The grass surface sits on rollers. Underneath is a concrete floor. The field can actually be rolled away so the stadium can hold concerts and other events.

BY THE NUMBERS

- The Cardinals' stadium has 63,400 seats and can expand to 78,600 seats.
- The stadium was built with enough concrete for a 900-mile stretch of sidewalk.
- The stadium's highest level of seats is known as the 400 level. It was designed to look like the nighttime sky.

The Cardinals' stadium is one of the most modern in the world.

Dressed for Success

Despite their many addresses, the Cardinals are a team that respects tradition. They have worn the same colors since they joined the NFL: black, white, and cardinal red. The team has featured its familiar *logo* since the 1940s. At first, the club used a red bird perched on a football. After the move to St. Louis, the team showed the cardinal running with a football under the city's famous Gateway Arch.

For many decades, the players wore plain white helmets. In 1960, the Cardinals began using a logo on the side of their helmets. It showed a cardinal with a fierce look in its eye. In 2005, the team changed the look on the bird's face to be even meaner. The Cardinals wanted their image to be a little tougher, so they made the bird appear that way, too.

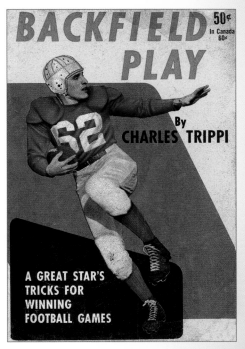

BACKFIELD PLAY

50¢
In Canada 60¢

By CHARLES TRIPPI

A GREAT STAR'S TRICKS FOR WINNING FOOTBALL GAMES

LEFT: Patrick Peterson wears the team's 2011 home uniform.
ABOVE: The equipment has changed a bit since the 1940s, but Charley Trippi's uniform color is the same bright red the Cardinals wear today.

We Won!

The first championship for the Cardinals came in 1925—and it was unexpected. Back then, the NFL team with the best record was crowned the league champ. In the 12th game of that season, the Cardinals met the Pottsville Maroons. Each team had nine victories. When the Maroons won, it appeared that they were headed for the NFL title.

However, weeks later, Pottsville's season was suspended after the team played an exhibition game against an all-star team in Philadelphia without the NFL's full permission. League rules said that a suspended team could not win the championship. So, the NFL awarded the title to the Cardinals. To this day, the official record books list the Cardinals as the 1925 NFL champs.

There was no doubt about the team's second championship. In 1947, coach Jimmy Conzelman had one of the league's most talented

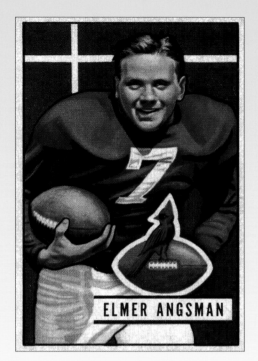

ELMER ANGSMAN

rosters. Paul Christman passed for more than 2,000 yards. His two best receivers, Mal Kutner and Bill Dewell, combined for 85 receptions. The team's rushing attack relied on Charley Trippi, Pat Harder, and Elmer Angsman. Together, they ran for more than 1,000 yards and scored 16 touchdowns. Harder was also one of the NFL's top kickers.

The Cardinals battled the crosstown Bears all season long for the **Western Division** title. They faced each other in the last game of the year. On the first play, Christman threw an 80-yard touchdown pass. The Cardinals never looked back. They won 30–21 and prepared to play the Philadelphia Eagles for the NFL championship.

The two teams met in Chicago on an icy field. Many of the Cardinals decided to wear sneakers instead of cleats to keep from slipping. In the first quarter, Trippi ran right through the Philadelphia defense for a 44-yard touchdown. In the second quarter, Angsman raced 70 yards for another score. Midway through the third quarter, Trippi caught a punt on his own 25-yard line and weaved through

the Philadelphia tacklers for an amazing touchdown. Angsman added a final score with his second 70-yard run of the day.

The Eagles, however, would not give up. Trailing by seven points in the fourth quarter, they drove down the field. Marshall Goldberg saved the day for the Cardinals with an **interception** that wrapped up the thrilling 28–21 victory. The Cardinals were champions of the NFL, and this time no one else could claim the league crown.

The Cardinals reached the title game again in 1948, but they lost in a rematch with the Eagles. It took 60 years before they got another shot at the championship again. By this time, the team had moved from Chicago to St. Louis to Arizona.

In 2008, veteran quarterback Kurt Warner teamed with receivers Larry Fitzgerald, Anquan Boldin, and Steve Breaston to give the

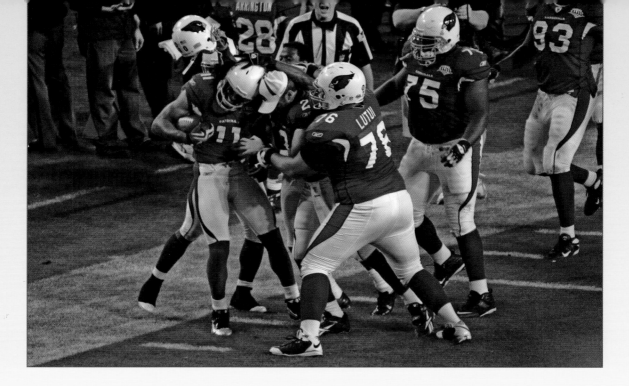

Cardinals a high-flying passing attack. The Cardinals won the NFC West and then tore through the playoffs to earn a spot in Super Bowl XLIII against the Pittsburgh Steelers. No one was happier than Bill Bidwill. His family had owned the Cardinals since the 1930s, and he had been running the team for nearly 50 years.

The game was a shootout from the opening kickoff. Warner and Fitzgerald connected for a touchdown with less than three minutes to go to give Arizona a 23–20 lead. Unfortunately, the defense could not hold the Steelers. With 35 seconds left, Pittsburgh scored a touchdown for a 27–23 victory. Arizona had fallen just short in its first Super Bowl, but everyone agreed it was a great game.

LEFT: Kurt Warner answers reporters' questions before the Super Bowl.
ABOVE: The team celebrates Larry Fitzgerald's go-ahead touchdown.

Go-To Guys

To be a true star in the NFL, you need more than fast feet and a big body. You have to be a "go-to guy"—someone the coach wants on the field at the end of a big game. Cardinals fans have had a lot to cheer about over the years, including these great stars ...

THE PIONEERS

PADDY DRISCOLL   Running Back/Quarterback/Kicker

• BORN: 1/11/1895   • DIED: 6/29/1968   • PLAYED FOR TEAM: 1920 TO 1925

Paddy Driscoll did it all for the Cardinals. His best weapon was his powerful right foot. Driscoll was a master punter and kicker. In 1922, he scored every point in two victories over the team's fiercest rival, the crosstown Bears.

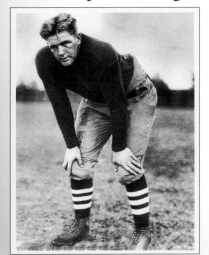

ERNIE NEVERS   Running Back

• BORN: 6/11/1903   • DIED: 5/3/1976
• PLAYED FOR TEAM: 1929 TO 1931

No one in the NFL had more talent or competed harder than Ernie Nevers. He was such a great athlete that he also played professional basketball and baseball. Nevers was voted into the **Hall of Fame** in 1963.

CHARLEY TRIPPI — Running Back/Defensive Back

- BORN: 12/14/1922 • PLAYED FOR TEAM: 1947 TO 1955

In 1947, the Cardinals signed Charley Trippi to a $100,000 contract—the highest ever for a football player at the time. He was worth the price. Trippi led the team to the NFL championship as a rookie and was named All-Pro the following year.

OLLIE MATSON — Running Back/Defensive Back

- BORN: 5/1/1930 • DIED: 2/19/2011 • PLAYED FOR TEAM: 1952 & 1954 TO 1958

Ollie Matson combined great power and speed to become one of the NFL's top players. He was voted All-Pro on defense in 1952 and on offense from 1954 to 1959. Matson was also the **Most Valuable Player (MVP)** of the 1956 Pro Bowl.

DICK LANE — Defensive Back

- BORN: 4/16/1928 • DIED: 1/29/2002 • PLAYED FOR TEAM: 1954 TO 1959

Dick Lane stuck to receivers like glue. In his first season with the Cardinals, he intercepted 10 passes. Lane was nicknamed "Night Train" after a famous song of the 1950s.

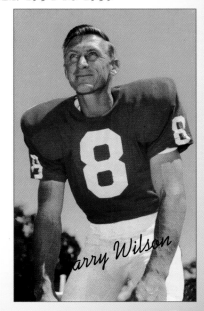

LARRY WILSON — Defensive Back

- BORN: 3/24/1938 • PLAYED FOR TEAM: 1960 TO 1972

Larry Wilson was a great all-around athlete. He was the master of the **safety blitz** and had 52 interceptions during his career. Wilson played in the Pro Bowl eight times.

LEFT: Ernie Nevers
RIGHT: Larry Wilson

JACKIE SMITH   Tight End

• BORN: 2/23/1940   • PLAYED FOR TEAM: 1963 TO 1977

A tight end must be able to catch passes and make blocks. Jackie Smith did both as well as anyone in the NFL. When Smith retired, he had more catches, yards, and touchdowns than any tight end in the game.

JIM HART   Quarterback

• BORN: 4/29/1944   • PLAYED FOR TEAM: 1966 TO 1983

Jim Hart was a strong-armed passer who became a star under coach Don Coryell. He went to the Pro Bowl each year from 1974 to 1977. Hart retired as the team's all-time leader in passing yards and touchdowns.

ROGER WEHRLI   Defensive Back

• BORN: 11/26/1947   • PLAYED FOR TEAM: 1969 TO 1982

Roger Wehrli was smart and fast. He studied opposing receivers and memorized their every move. Wehrli was named All-Pro each season from 1975 to 1977.

DAN DIERDORF   Offensive Lineman

• BORN: 6/29/1949   • PLAYED FOR TEAM: 1971 TO 1983

Dan Dierdorf was very *agile* for a man his size. He could blast open holes for running backs or stop pass-rushers from reaching the quarterback. The Cardinals gave up the fewest **sacks** in the NFC five years in a row with Dierdorf leading the offensive line.

AENEAS WILLIAMS Defensive Back

- BORN: 1/29/1968   • PLAYED FOR TEAM: 1991 TO 2000

Aeneas Williams used his strength and speed to shut down receivers. Opposing quarterbacks learned quickly that it was a bad idea to throw his way. In 10 seasons with the Cardinals, Williams had 46 interceptions and ran back six of them for touchdowns.

ADRIAN WILSON Defensive Back

- BORN: 10/12/1979   • FIRST YEAR WITH TEAM: 2001

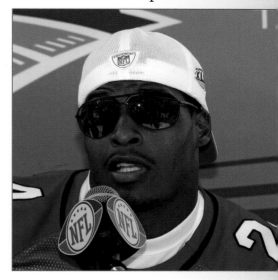

Adrian Wilson's great size, speed, and jumping ability made him one of the best all-around defensive players in the NFL. In 2005, he set a record for safeties with eight sacks. A year later, he returned a fumble 99 yards for a touchdown. Wilson was picked to play in the Pro Bowl five times from 2006 to 2011.

LARRY FITZGERALD Receiver

- BORN: 8/31/1983   • FIRST YEAR WITH TEAM: 2004

Larry Fitzgerald was a mismatch for anyone who tried to cover him. He was too big and strong for smaller defensive backs, and linebackers couldn't keep up with his speed. Fitzgerald led the NFL with 103 catches in 2005. In his first eight seasons, he had 73 touchdown receptions and made the Pro Bowl six times.

LEFT: Roger Wehrli
ABOVE: Adrian Wilson talks to reporters before Super Bowl XLIII.

Calling the Shots

© Gary Thomas

O ver their long history, the Cardinals have had some of football's greatest coaches. Included on that list are Paddy Driscoll, Guy Chamberlin, Ernie Nevers, Curly Lambeau, Joe Stydahar, Wally Lemm, Bud Wilkinson, Buddy Ryan, and Dennis Green. They all ranked among the best in the business.

The only coach to guide the team to a championship was Jimmy Conzelman. He had been a star in the early days of the NFL, and he knew what it took to build a winner. In the years after World War II, he convinced team owner Charley Bidwill to assemble a "dream backfield" of Paul Christman, Charley Trippi, Pat Harder, Elmer Angsman, and Marshall Goldberg. Conzelman built his offense around them, and the Cardinals won the 1947 NFL championship.

In the 1970s, it looked as if the Cardinals might challenge for a title under Don Coryell.

LEFT: This postcard shows Jimmy Conzelman as a coach.
RIGHT: Ken Whisenhunt does an interview before Super Bowl XLIII.

He loved to pass the ball and encouraged quarterback Jim Hart to make use of his speedy receivers. When opponents geared their defense to stop Hart, Coryell crossed them up by getting the ball to running back Terry Metcalf. In 1974 and 1975, the Cardinals won the NFC East, but they lost in the playoffs both seasons.

The team reached the **postseason** again under Jim Hanifan in 1982 and in 1998 under Vince Tobin. However, it was not until Ken Whisenhunt became head coach in 2007 that the Cardinals turned into true *contenders* again. Like Coryell, Whisenhunt believed the quickest way to the end zone came through the air. In his second season in charge, he led the team on an amazing run through the playoffs. For the first time ever, the Cardinals won the NFC championship.

One Great Day

The 2008 NFL season was full of surprises. None was bigger than the performance of the Cardinals. It had been 10 years since Arizona had enjoyed a winning season, so expectations for the team were low. The Cardinals rode a great passing attack to first place in the NFC West with a 9–7 record. Still, when the playoffs started, most experts predicted a quick exit for Arizona.

The Cardinals had a different idea. They won their first two postseason games to set up a showdown with the Philadelphia Eagles in the **NFC Championship Game**. More than 70,000 fans filled Arizona's stadium to cheer on their team.

The Cardinals got off to a great start on a touchdown pass from Kurt Warner to Larry Fitzgerald. The pair connected again a few minutes later, this time on a 62-yard scoring strike. With three minutes left in the first half, Warner and Fitzgerald made it three touchdowns. Neil Rackers added a **field goal** on the final play of the second quarter, and the Cardinals went into the locker room leading 24–6.

Tim Hightower barrels into a tackler during the
NFC Championship Game.

The Eagles did not give up easily. Philadelphia crept back into the game, cutting Arizona's lead to 24–19. Early in the fourth quarter, the Eagles scored on a long pass play, and suddenly the Cardinals were trailing 25–24.

Arizona started its next drive on its own 26-yard line. Warner moved the team down the field, but the drive looked like it would stall. On a key fourth down, Tim Hightower ran for a first down to keep the Cardinals alive. Moments later, Warner threw a pass to Hightower for the go-ahead touchdown. Arizona added a **two-point conversion** to make the final score 32–25. The Cardinals and their fans celebrated their unexpected NFC championship.

Legend Has It

Who was the bravest Cardinal?

LEGEND HAS IT that Pat Tillman was. Tillman was a hard-hitting defensive back who played for the Cardinals from 1998 to 2001. He gave 100 percent on every play and inspired his teammates to do the same. Tillman was also very patriotic. After the terror attacks of September 11, 2001, he enlisted in the United States Army. He was killed in action in the mountains of Afghanistan in 2004. The Cardinals honored Tillman by retiring his number in 2006.

ABOVE: Pat Tillman

Was Bobby Joe Green the last NFL player to take the field without a facemask?

LEGEND HAS IT that it he was. Green was the punter for the Cardinals in the 1960s and early 1970s. Players who joined the NFL after 1954 had to wear facemasks—that was the rule. But the rule did not apply to "part-time" players such as punters. Green played for 14 years without any protection for his face and retired after the 1973 season.

Who had the worst day ever for a quarterback?

LEGEND HAS IT that Jim Hardy did. Hardy became the Cardinals' quarterback in 1949. He set an NFL record by throwing 114 passes in a row without an interception. However, in a game against the Philadelphia Eagles in 1950, Hardy could barely complete a pass to his teammates. The Eagles intercepted eight passes, and he also **fumbled** twice—and both led to Philadelphia touchdowns! Hardy did not let that game bother him. The next week, he threw six touchdown passes in a victory over the Baltimore Colts.

As the Cardinals prepared for the 1920 season, they faced some stiff competition. That year, there was a second team in Chicago, the Tigers. Both clubs had paid $100 to join the American Professional Football Association (APFA).

There was concern among some people that Chicago could not support two professional football teams. The APFA owners got together and agreed that either the Cardinals or the Tigers would have to go out of business at the end of the season. The teams were scheduled to play each other in November. The winner would stay in the league, and the loser would fold.

The Tigers had some very good players, including Emmett Keefe, Guil Falcon, and Milt Ghee. The Cardinals had Paddy Driscoll and not much else—but that was

enough. Driscoll was one of the most talented players of his era. Against the Tigers, he had a great game. In fact, Driscoll scored the only points in the game when he broke free for a 40-yard touchdown run. The Cardinals won, 6–0.

Afterward, the Cardinals and their fans celebrated into the night. No one was happier than Driscoll. The Cardinals paid him $300 a game, which was a lot of money back then. Driscoll was thankful that his paychecks would keep coming.

Many people thought the Cardinals were crazy to spend that much on one player, but it turned out to be a wise investment. Some years later, the team owners sold the Cardinals for $50,000. They owed a big *thank-you* to Driscoll. If he had not been on the field that day against the Tigers, the Cardinals might not exist today!

Team Spirit

The Cardinals have always had a close bond with their fans. That's saying a lot since the team has had three homes during its long history. Fans throughout the Southwest were overjoyed when the Cardinals came to Arizona. Football is very popular in this part of the country, and the people of the region were hungry for an NFL team. The Cardinals were an answer to their prayers.

The Cardinals make a special point of reaching out to their young fans. Before each game, one child is picked from the crowd to accompany the team captains to midfield for the official coin toss. Kids can also test themselves on a special skills course at the stadium.

Like many NFL teams, the Cardinals have their own cheerleading squad. They have a junior cheer squad, too. The Arizona *mascot* is Big Red, a cardinal with a wingspan of seven feet. He visits schools around the state during the year.

LEFT: Red is always the color of the day at Arizona games.
ABOVE: Fans bought this pin the year the team moved from St. Louis, when the club was known as the Phoenix Cardinals.

n this timeline, each Super Bowl is listed under the year it was played. Remember that the Super Bowl is held early in the year and is actually part of the previous season. For example, Super Bowl XLVI was played on February 5, 2012, but it was the championship of the 2011 NFL season.

1925
The Cardinals win the NFL championship.

1954
Dick "Night Train" Lane leads the league with 10 interceptions.

1920
The Cardinals play their first season in the APFA.

1947
The Cardinals win their second NFL championship.

1960
The team moves to St. Louis.

The Cardinals try to stay dry during the 1947 title game.

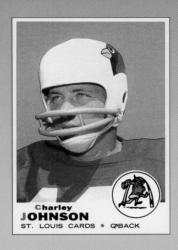

Charley
Johnson

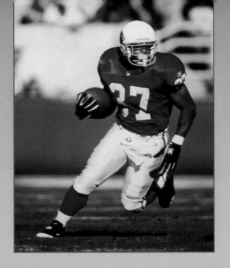

Larry
Centers

1964
Charley Johnson leads
the NFL with 3,045
passing yards.

1996
Larry Centers makes
the Pro Bowl for the
second year in a row.

2009
The Cardinals play in
Super Bowl XLIII.

1975
Terry Metcalf and Jim Otis
both play in the Pro Bowl.

1986
Vai Sikahema is named
All-Pro as a rookie.

2011
Patrick Peterson
returns four punts
for touchdowns.

Terry
Metcalf

Fun Facts

GRAY AREA

From 1973 to 1982, Mel Gray caught a pass in 121 games in a row. In 12 seasons with the Cardinals, he averaged 18.9 yards per catch.

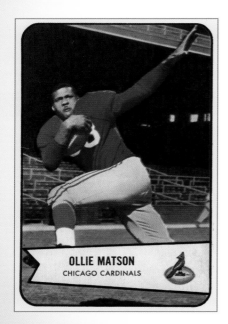

OLLIE MATSON
CHICAGO CARDINALS

FAST START

When Ollie Matson began his rookie season for the Cardinals in 1952, he was already world-famous. A few weeks earlier, Matson had won silver and bronze medals in the *Olympics* as a sprinter for the United States.

RARE ROOKIE

On his first play with the Cardinals in 2011, Patrick Peterson intercepted a pass and ran it back for a touchdown in a preseason game. In his first game of the regular season that year, Peterson set a team record by returning a punt for an 89-yard touchdown.

ABOVE: Ollie Matson
RIGHT: Neil Lomax

PASSING GRADES

The Cardinals have had two of the best single-game passing performances in NFL history—and both came against the Washington Redskins. In a 1984 game, Neil Lomax set a team record with 468 yards. Boomer Esiason topped that mark in 1996 with 522 yards.

POST POSITION

In the 2008 playoffs and Super Bowl XLIII, Larry Fitzgerald set a postseason record with 30 catches, 546 receiving yards, and seven touchdowns. Fitzgerald also caught two touchdown passes in the Pro Bowl that winter and was named MVP of the game.

GIVE THE BALL TO GUS

The team's best player in the late 1930s was Gus Tinsley. He set an NFL record with a 97-yard touchdown catch in 1937. Tinsley broke his own record in 1938 with a 98-yard touchdown. He left the team a year later to coach a high school football team.

Talking Football

"I've got confidence in myself, my teammates, and my quarterback. If a team is going to give us one-on-one coverage, we're going to go at it, no matter who it is."

▶ **Roy Green,** *on his ability to beat any defender*

"No matter what happens on the football field, it doesn't change the kind of person I am."

▶ **Kurt Warner,** *on separating his career from his personal life*

"We are just lucky to have a very good player like that on our team."

▶ **Ken Whisenhunt,** *on Larry Fitzgerald*

"We're right where we want to be."

▶ **Larry Fitzgerald,** *on the future of the Cardinals*

"No one knew how to say *Aeneas*, so I wanted a name like Ralph or Joe. But as I got older, after people started learning how to pronounce it, I enjoyed it."

▶ **Aeneas Williams**, *on his unusual first name*

"His competitiveness was his strength and he had a feel for the game, a real nose for the ball."

▶ **Bill Bidwill**, *on Larry Wilson*

"He was the greatest competitor I ever played with. He refused to run out of bounds to avoid a tackle, even if it meant getting crushed."

▶ **Charley Trippi**, *on teammate Pat Harder*

"I want to do something extraordinary, not just make a tackle. I want to make people's eyes widen."

▶ **Simeon Rice**, *on his desire to be a star*

LEFT: Roy Green
ABOVE: Aeneas Williams

Great Debates

People who root for the Cardinals love to compare their favorite moments, teams, and players. Some debates have been going on for years! How would you settle these classic football arguments?

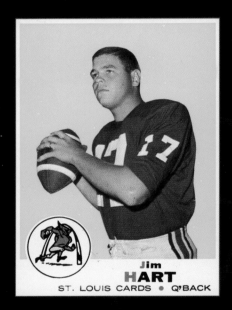

Jim
HART
ST. LOUIS CARDS • Q'BACK

Jim Hart was the team's greatest player ....

… because the numbers say so. He holds the team records for completions, passing yards, touchdowns, the longest pass, and the most game-winning drives. Hart (LEFT) was the most popular Cardinal when they played in St. Louis, and he also is popular in Chicago and Arizona—even though he never played in those places!

Sorry. No Cardinal can compare to Ollie Matson ....

… because he was an All-Pro in five of his six seasons with the team. Matson was the fastest player in the NFL during the 1950s. He was usually among the league leaders in rushing yards, kick and punt returns, and touchdowns. What more could you ask from the best player on the team? Oh, one more thing—Matson played defense, too!

The 1947 Cardinals would beat the 2008 Cardinals …

… because they had a high-powered offense and a tough defense. Their All-Pro blockers would push around the 2008 team's defensive line. Pat Harder, Charley Trippi, and Elmer Angsman would grind out one first down after another. If the 1947 team needed to complete a pass, Paul Christman had a pair of sure-handed receivers in Billy Dewell and Mal Kutner. The same guys starred on defense, along with Red Cochran and Marshall Goldberg.

Are you serious? The 2008 Cardinals would chase the 1947 team off the field …

… because they were so athletic. Larry Fitzgerald and Anquan Boldin looked more like linebackers than receivers, and Steve Breaston (RIGHT) had breathtaking speed. On defense, Karlos Dansby and Adrian Wilson roamed all over the field to make tackles. The 2008 team also had a secret weapon in Neil Rackers. He missed just three field goals all season long.

T he great Cardinals teams and players have left their marks on the record books. These are the "best of the best" …

Ollie Matson

CARDINALS AWARD WINNERS

WINNER	AWARD	YEAR
Ollie Matson	Pro Bowl MVP	1956
Johnny Roland	Rookie of the Year	1966
Dale Meinert	Pro Bowl co-MVP	1966
Don Coryell	Coach of the Year	1974
Ottis Anderson	Offensive Rookie of the Year	1979
Simeon Rice	Defensive Rookie of the Year	1996
Anquan Boldin	Offensive Rookie of the Year	2003
Larry Fitzgerald	Pro Bowl MVP	2008

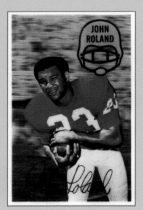

Johnny Roland

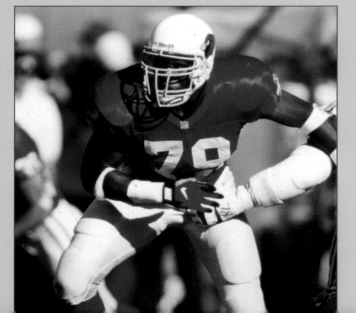

Simeon Rice

CARDINALS ACHIEVEMENTS

ACHIEVEMENT	YEAR
NFL Champions	1925
Western Division Champions	1947
NFL Champions	1947
Western Division Champions	1948
NFC East Champions	1974
NFC East Champions	1975
NFC West Champions	2008
NFC Champions	2008
NFC West Champions	2009

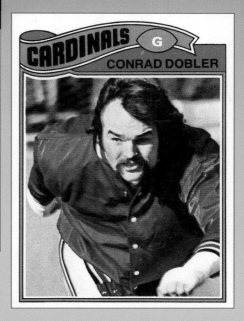

TOP RIGHT: Conrad Dobler starred for the Cardinals in the 1970s.
BOTTOM RIGHT: Dominique Rodgers-Cromartie led the 2008 NFC champions in interceptions.
BELOW: Bill Bidwill has owned the Cardinals since 1962.

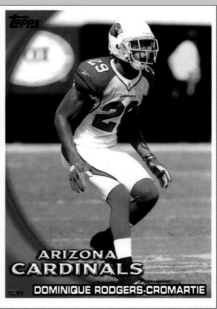

Pinpoints

The history of a football team is made up of many smaller stories. These stories take place all over the map—not just in the city a team calls "home." Match the pushpins on these maps to the **Team Facts**, and you will begin to see the story of the Cardinals unfold!

1. Glendale, Arizona—*The Cardinals have played in the Glendale-Phoenix area since 1988.*
2. Fresno, California—*Mel Gray was born here.*
3. Seattle, Washington—*Terry Metcalf was born here.*
4. Rigby, Idaho—*Larry Wilson was born here.*
5. Trinity, Texas—*Ollie Matson was born here.*
6. Minneapolis, Minnesota—*Larry Fitzgerald was born here.*
7. Madison, Wisconsin—*Jim Bakken was born here.*
8. Akron, Ohio—*Beanie Wells was born here.*
9. Chicago, Illinois—*The Cardinals played here from 1920 to 1959.*
10. St. Louis, Missouri—*The Cardinals played here from 1960 to 1987.*
11. Fort Lauderdale, Florida—*Patrick Peterson was born here.*
12. Nuku'alofa, Tonga—*Vai Sikahema was born here.*

Mel Gray

Glossary

👥 *AGILE*—Quick and graceful.

🧠 **ALL-PRO**—An honor given to the best players at their positions at the end of each season.

🧠 **AMERICAN PROFESSIONAL FOOTBALL ASSOCIATION (APFA)**—The league that started in 1920 and later became the NFL.

👥 *CONTENDERS*—People or teams that compete for a championship.

👥 *DECADE*—A period of 10 years; also specific periods, such as the 1950s.

🧠 **EAST DIVISION**—A group of teams that play in the eastern part of the country.

👥 *ENTHUSIASM*—Strong excitement.

🧠 **FIELD GOAL**—A goal from the field, kicked over the crossbar and between the goal posts. A field goal is worth three points.

🧠 **FUMBLED**—Dropped the ball.

🧠 **HALL OF FAME**—The museum in Canton, Ohio, where football's greatest players are honored.

🧠 **INTERCEPTION**—A pass that is caught by the defensive team.

👥 *LOGO*—A symbol or design that represents a company or team.

👥 *MASCOT*—An animal or person believed to bring a group good luck.

🧠 **MOST VALUABLE PLAYER (MVP)**—The award given each year to the league's best player; also given to the best player in the Super Bowl and Pro Bowl.

🧠 **NATIONAL FOOTBALL CONFERENCE (NFC)**—One of two groups of teams that make up the NFL.

🧠 **NATIONAL FOOTBALL LEAGUE (NFL)**—The league that started in 1920 and is still operating today.

🧠 **NFC CHAMPIONSHIP GAME**—The game played to determine which NFC team will go to the Super Bowl.

🧠 **NFC WEST**—A division for teams that play in the western part of the country.

👥 *OLYMPICS*—An international sports competition held every four years.

🧠 **PLAYOFFS**—The games played after the regular season to determine which teams play in the Super Bowl.

🧠 **POSTSEASON**—Another term for playoffs.

🧠 **PRO BOWL**—The NFL's all-star game, played after the regular season.

👥 *PROFESSIONAL*—Paid to play.

👥 *RETRACTABLE*—Able to be pulled back.

👥 *RIVALRIES*—Extremely emotional competitions.

🧠 **ROLE PLAYERS**—People who are asked to do specific things when they are in a game.

🧠 **ROOKIE**—A player in his first year.

🧠 **SACKS**—Tackles of the quarterback behind the line of scrimmage.

🧠 **SAFETY BLITZ**—A defensive play in which a safety blasts through the offensive line on the snap of the ball.

🧠 **SUPER BOWL**—The championship of the NFL, played between the winners of the National Football Conference and American Football Conference.

👥 *TRADITION*—A belief or custom that is handed down from generation to generation.

🧠 **TWO-POINT CONVERSION**—A play following a touchdown where the offense tries to cross the goal line with the ball from the 2-yard line, instead of kicking an extra point.

🧠 **WESTERN DIVISION**—A group of teams that play in the western part of the country.

👥 *WORLD WAR II*—The war among the major powers of Europe, Asia, and North America that lasted from 1939 to 1945. The United States entered the war in 1941.

OVERTIME

TEAM SPIRIT introduces a great way to stay up to date with your team! Visit our **OVERTIME** link and get connected to the latest and greatest updates. **OVERTIME** serves as a young reader's ticket to an exclusive web page—with more stories, fun facts, team records, and photos of the Cardinals. Content is updated during and after each season. The **OVERTIME** feature also enables readers to send comments and letters to the author! Log onto:

www.norwoodhousepress.com/library.aspx

and click on the tab: **TEAM SPIRIT** to access **OVERTIME**.

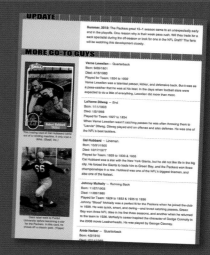

Read all the books in the series to learn more about professional sports. For a complete listing of the baseball, basketball, football, and hockey teams in the **TEAM SPIRIT** series, visit our website at:

www.norwoodhousepress.com/library.aspx

On the Road

ARIZONA CARDINALS
1 Cardinals Drive
Glendale, Arizona 85305
602-379-0101
www.azcardinals.com

THE PRO FOOTBALL HALL OF FAME
2121 George Halas Drive NW
Canton, Ohio 44708
330-456-8207
www.profootballhof.com

On the Bookshelf

To learn more about the sport of football, look for these books at your library or bookstore:

- Frederick, Shane. *The Best of Everything Football Book.* North Mankato, Minnesota: Capstone Press, 2011.

- Jacobs, Greg. *The Everything Kids' Football Book: The All-Time Greats, Legendary Teams, Today's Superstars—And Tips on Playing Like a Pro.* Avon, Massachusetts: Adams Media Corporation, 2010.

- Editors of *Sports Illustrated for Kids. 1st and 10: Top 10 Lists of Everything in Football.* New York, New York: Sports Illustrated Books, 2011.

Index

About the Author

MARK STEWART has written more than 50 books on football and over 150 sports books for kids. He grew up in New York City during the 1960s rooting for the Giants and Jets, and was lucky enough to meet players from both teams. Mark comes from a family of writers. His grandfather was Sunday Editor of *The New York Times,* and his mother was Articles Editor of *Ladies' Home Journal* and *McCall's.* Mark has profiled hundreds of athletes over the past 25 years. He has also written several books about his native New York and New Jersey, his home today. Mark is a graduate of Duke University, with a degree in history. He lives and works in a home overlooking Sandy Hook, New Jersey. You can contact Mark through the Norwood House Press website.